APOLLO 13

Houston, We have a Problem!

Robyn P. Watts

KNOWLEDGE BOOKS

Teacher Notes:

This story explains NASA's Apollo Space Program to get a 'Man on the Moon' and the challenges they faced along the way, including the incredible survival of the Apollo 13 crew in the face of disaster. It is an incredible story of scientific achievement, human tenacity, and resilience.

Discussion Points for consideration:

1. NASA had a huge team working together on the Apollo Space Program. How important was teamwork and communication to them? Give examples.

2. Astronauts train for many years before going on missions. Discuss the pros and cons of being an astronaut.

3. The Apollo 13 astronauts had to quickly problem-solve to save themselves and the mission. What did they do and how hard would this have been for them?

Sight words, difficult to decode words, and infrequent words to be introduced and practised before reading this book: astronauts, atmosphere, communication, measurement, carbon dioxide, massive, information, colliding, kilometres, something, enormous, mighty, electricity, equipment, squeeze, radiation, Apollo, mission, instruments, combined, material, engineering, fumes, location, altitude.

Contents

1

This is the amazing story of Apollo 13. It was the Moon shot that went wrong. It was made into a movie starring Tom Hanks. See p.3 QR code.

The Apollo program was a series of Moon missions run by NASA. Their goal was to put people on the Moon. Apollo 11 was the first to land people on the Moon.

The USA and the Russians were in a space race. The Russians had put the lunar lander on the Moon. They were way ahead of the USA. In 1961, USA's President John F. Kennedy said they would put a man on the moon before 1970.

1. The Moon

The Moon formed just after the Earth. It is thought to be rocks and dust from the Earth colliding with a large planet. The Moon is thought to be rocks thrown out into space because of this collision.

Moon rocks brought back to Earth show it to be very old. The Moon orbits the Earth. It shows the same face towards the Earth. The other side facing away from Earth is the dark side of the Moon. The Moon controls the tides on the Earth.

The Moon moves around the Earth at a distance of about 221,000 miles. The Moon is about a quarter of the size of Earth. It has no air or atmosphere.

2. Saturn V Rocket "The Beast"

Early rockets all had the same idea: to get something up into space. To get the rocket into space, it needs to go very fast so that it enters an orbit around the Earth.

Rockets took a long time to control properly. Computers are used to stop the rocket getting off track.

The rocket power needed to get a capsule into space is enormous. It has to be a massive rocket to get the spacecraft to the Moon. The Saturn V Rocket was used for a super heavy lift.

It is a mighty scene to watch it take off. It uses 3,000 tons of rocket fuel and flames spew out for 20-30 seconds. It was the called *'The Beast'*!

3. Earth Escape Speed

Escaping the Earth is not easy. If you throw a ball in the air it falls back. That is gravity. If you hurl a rocket up in the air it will come back to Earth.

The escape speed is how fast a rocket needs to go to get out of Earth's pull. This speed will then let it start to orbit the Earth. It then becomes a satellite. To escape Earth, it needs a speed of 7 miles per second. This is over 13,000 miles in an hour.

If it goes any slower, it starts to be pulled back to Earth. Gravity pulls the slowing rocket back to Earth. The rocket must go very fast to be able to stay in orbit around the Earth.

4. Journey to the Moon

Apollo 11 was the first to land on the Moon. It took a lot of difficult maths and physics to figure out how to land on the Moon.

The first thing is to get into space. You need a command capsule to get back to Earth and a services module to hold all the fuel, electricity, oxygen, and equipment. Then you need a Moon lander. So instead of just the capsule going around the Earth as a satellite, you need to have a Moon lander and a cabin to hold all the gear.

All of the fuel, oxygen, food, and equipment weighed over 43 tons. This image is of the lunar lander, command capsule, and the services module.

11

5. Command Capsule

The command capsule is small - it is like being inside a small car. You squeeze in the top and there is not much room to move. The command capsule sits at the top of the rocket. This is the capsule you use to return to Earth.

You must be well-trained as a test pilot and be able to put up with the strong G-forces of the rocket taking off. You also need to be able to do all the important jobs and repairs.

The Apollo 11 mission took 9 days. From lift off to return to Earth, it was a long time in space making sure everything was done properly.

You train and practise to make sure everything is done quickly.

6. Apollo Moon Missions

Apollo 1 had a fire which killed all 3 astronauts. The astronauts were doing tests when the module caught fire. By the time they got to the astronauts, they had died from burns and fumes.

Apollo 4 and 5 were not crewed. These flights were to test the command capsule and the lunar module.

Apollo 6 carried the lunar module and the command space module. Apollo 13 was the third crewed mission to go to the Moon. The Apollo missions before Apollo 11 were testing to get to the Moon. Some had crew but Apollo 11 was the first one to land on the Moon.

Apollo 7 had a crew and went around the Earth for 7 days. It tested the command service module systems.

Apollo 8 went on and orbited the Moon. The astronauts made 10 orbits of the Moon before returning to Earth.

Apollo 9 tested the docking and lunar module again.

Apollo 10 travelled above the Moon and tested the lunar module. Apollo 10 did not land on the Moon.

Apollo 11 was the first crew to land on the Moon. They landed on the Moon and spent 21 hours there. This was followed by returning to the command capsule and going back to Earth.

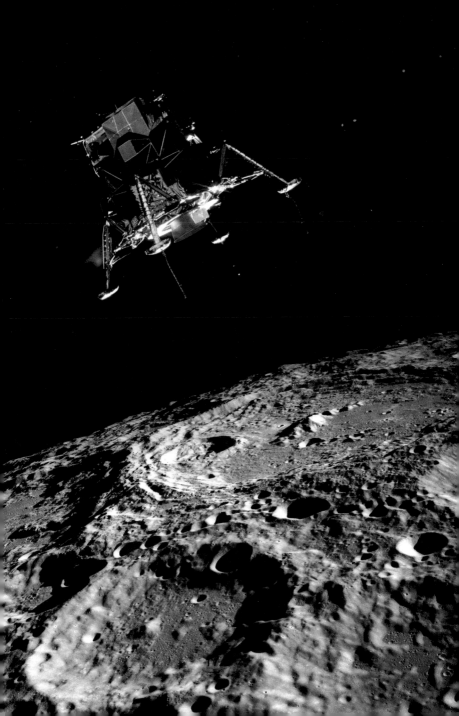

7. Apollo 13 Mission

Apollo 13 was the same process as Apollo 11 and 12, but this time they would explore further from the lunar lander. The commander was James Lovell, the lunar module pilot was Fred Haise, and the command module pilot was John Swigert.

Apollo 13 was going to land near some mountains on the Moon, just next to a crater.

The spacesuits contain many features. The suits weigh 40 pounds and are very heavy to wear. In space it does not matter because you are weightless.

Pockets on the spacesuits contain equipment such as radiation meters, pencils, and a sandwich for lunch.

The space suit is hooked up to oxygen and air tanks so they can breathe and stay cool when in space. The astronauts breathe 100% oxygen when beginning the flight.

Getting into the capsule requires some help. You have a big spacesuit on, and you are being pushed into a tiny area. The astronauts are loaded into the command module by ground crew.

Once inside and seated in their chairs, they are hooked up. Air goes throughout their suits to keep them cool. Oxygen is fed into the cabin for use during the flight. For more details, scan the QR code on the next page.

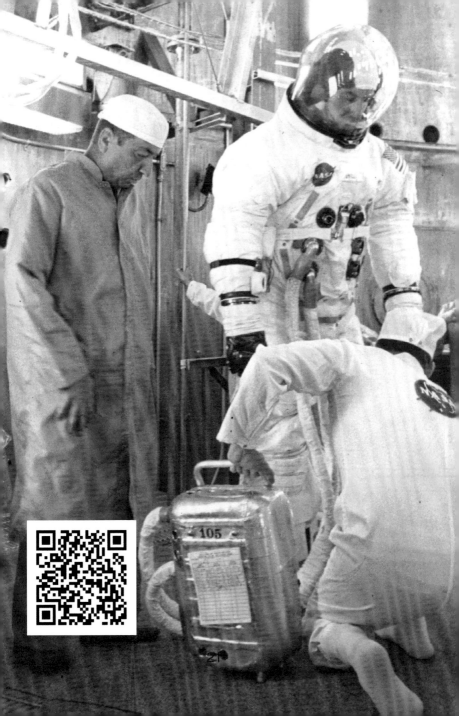

It requires many years of training to understand how to run all parts of the spacecraft. The control panel looks very difficult. There are lots of switches and meters measuring and controlling the spacecraft. Some of these switches are used once and then not touched. All the systems are managed from this master display console.

For about 90 minutes the astronauts go through all the checks and testing. All the switches and panels are checked before lift-off. Once these checks are completed, then the mission is ready to launch.

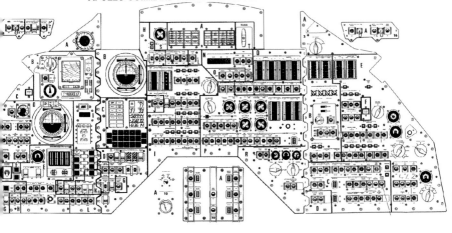

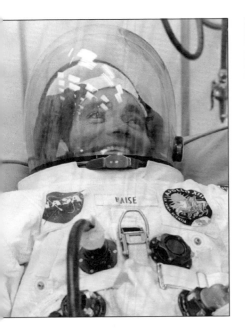

Launch Control Room is where all the engineers are checking the rocket and the crew. This is based at the launch site. The crews fitting the astronauts start to close and move back from the rocket. This is about 45 minutes before launch.

The Launch Control hands over to the Mission Control after the spacecraft leaves the launchpad.

At about 60 seconds before launch, all the power is switched on. The next step is to fire up the rockets. This is called the ignition and is like using a lighter to start a big explosion.

The Mission Control Center takes control of the spacecraft after it is launched. About 42 miles up in space, the big Stage 1 rocket falls away, and the other rocket starts using fuel.

The rocket is not travelling straight up. This is to match the way it leaves the Earth's atmosphere. This will take it on an orbit of the Earth.

The Tower Jett is over the nose of the command capsule. It looks like a needle at the top. This protects the command capsule during launch. The Tower Jett is now pushed away as it is no longer needed.

The spacecraft is now over 93 miles above ground and is travelling at over 2 miles per second. It needs to keep going faster to break out of the atmosphere and orbit. It needs to be over 4.5 miles per second, otherwise it cannot orbit the Earth.

The engines are still burning fuel to increase speed. The fuel is totally used up in the next stage before dumping the third stage of the rocket.

This then brings the spacecraft into orbit around the Earth. It has nearly reached a speed where it will now orbit the Earth at the right speed to stay in orbit. If it was too slow it would fall back to Earth.

The next stage of the Moon mission is to get out of Earth's orbit and head to the Moon. This requires further effort on the part of the rockets.

The cabin is now under pressure with oxygen, so the astronauts can take off their heavy space helmets and gloves. The astronauts are weightless and can float in the cabin. They need to be careful as moving your head suddenly can make you feel sick. They also need to be careful not to bump any switches.

The astronauts are very high up now. They can see the Atlantic Ocean, thunder and lightning, and the air glowing beneath them.

They would continue to orbit the Earth unless they push the spacecraft further out of orbit. Once it goes further away from the Earth, the Moon's gravity attracts the spacecraft. The Moon then is a stronger source of gravity and the spacecraft will head into an orbit of the Moon.

To get into the Moon's orbit it needs to start the booster rockets to push the spacecraft out of Earth's gravity.

The computers on board plot their speed, location, and altitude. This is combined with other instruments to help them know exactly where they are located. This helps the astronauts make sure they are on course exactly as required.

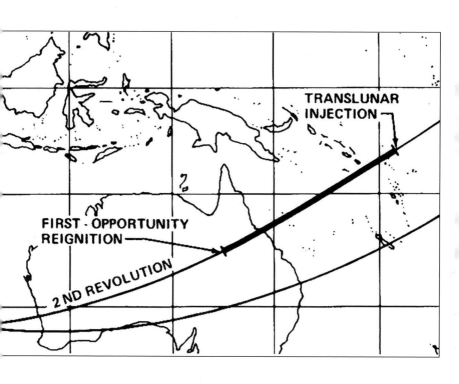

TRANSLUNAR
INJECTION

FIRST - OPPORTUNITY
REIGNITION

2 ND REVOLUTION

The spacecraft is on its way to the Moon. The rocket tanks are started for about 5-6 minutes which pushes the spacecraft into an orbit towards the Moon. Apollo 13 is on its second orbit of the Earth and has been in space for 2 hours 45 minutes. Apollo 13 is now heading to orbit the Moon.

Apollo 13 has ditched the last rocket tanks. It can now connect with the lunar landing module. To do this, it must separate from the second stage and turn in space. The lunar module is joined with the command capsule.

This will allow the astronauts to climb into the lunar lander when it is time to go to the surface of the moon.

First, the panels and the rocket booster are removed. These are blown with charges and the lunar lander can be seen.

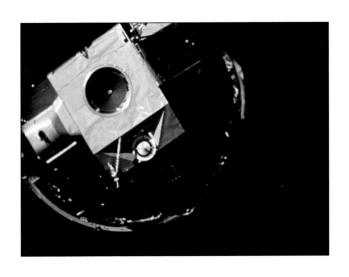

The door hatch is at the top of the command module. It is easier to do a spin of the lunar module than have two doors in the command module.

Once the lunar lander is connected, it is now ready for the lunar landing. The crew can now climb through the hatch.

It is time to go through all the checks and reviews. The Apollo 13 is leaving Earth towards the Moon. These are images taken on board. It is now 9 hours since take-off.

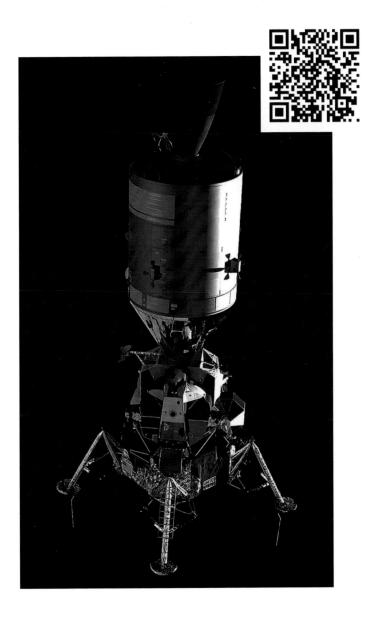

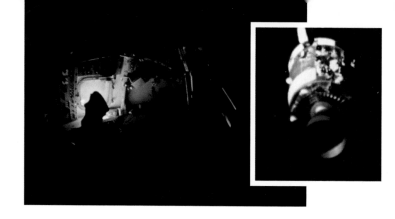

8. We Have a Problem

Almost 187,000 miles away from Earth and about 56 hours into the flight, they needed to check the oxygen tanks. This meant a stir of the tanks. This caused an explosion which blew the tank and damaged some of the batteries. The service module was damaged very badly.

A decision was made to move into the lunar module to save power for communication and getting back to the Earth.

9. Returning to Earth 'Slingshot'

The inside temperature of the lunar module was about 37 degrees Fahrenheit. The oxygen levels in the air were dropping, and bad gases were building up.

The crew had to work on ways to purify the air. This was solved with a simple filter. This cleaned the carbon dioxide out of the air.

Apollo 13 used the Moon's gravity to orbit it again and then head out towards Earth. This is a 'Slingshot' orbit to get the speed to return to Earth.

Once the lunar module reached the Earth's orbit, the astronauts climbed back into the command module and closed the hatch. The lunar module was then cut off to float away.

The re-entry to the Earth used measurements to work out the line of entry. It had to be correct, otherwise it would go too fast and go back into orbit. If it was too steep it could burn up. The command module heats up as it hits the atmosphere.

Everything worked perfectly. They splashed down in the ocean. Apollo 13 was very lucky!

Word Bank

astronauts

atmosphere

communication

measurement

carbon dioxide

massive

information

colliding

something

enormous

mighty

electricity

equipment

squeeze

radiation

Apollo

mission

instruments

combined

material

engineering

fumes

location

altitude